21st Century Skills Library

CAMPAIGN STRATEGY

Cherry Lake Press

by Samantha Bell

Cherry Lake Press

Published in the United States of America by
Cherry Lake Publishing Group
Ann Arbor, Michigan
www.cherrylakepublishing.com

Reading Adviser: Beth Walker Gambro, MS, Ed., Reading Consultant, Yorkville, IL

Content Adviser: Mark Richards, Ph.D., Professor, Dept. of Political Science,
Grand Valley State University, Allendale, MI

Photo Credits: © AP Photo/Charles Rex Arbogast, cover, title page; © wavebreakmedia/Shutterstock, 5; © Rawpixel.com/Shutterstock, 7; © Jose Gil/Shutterstock, 8; © Andrey_Popov/Shutterstock, 10; © Joseph Sohm/Shutterstock, 11; © George Sheldon/Shutterstock, 13; Tony Webster from Minneapolis, Minnesota, United States, CC BY 2.0 via Wikimedia Commons, 14; © Trong Nguyen/Shutterstock, 15; Harris & Ewing Collection, Prints and Photographs Division, Library of Congress, 17; Karsten Sethre from Austin, TX, CC BY-SA 2.0 via Wikimedia Commons, 18; © Juli Hansen/Shutterstock, 21; © JRdes/Shutterstock, 23; © wellphoto/Shutterstock, 24; © Tero Vesalainen/Shutterstock, 25; © DimaBerlin/Shutterstock, 26; Amaury Laporte, CC BY 2.0 via Wikimedia Commons, 29; A McLin, CC BY 2.0 via Wikimedia Commons, 30; © Rebekah Zemansky/Shutterstock, 31; © Solphoto/Shutterstock, 33; © Nopparat Khokthong/Shutterstock, 34; © Wangkun Jia/Shutterstock, 37; Amidamelio, CC BY-SA 4.0 via Wikimedia Commons, 38; Evan Guest, CC BY 2.0 via Wikimedia Commons, 39; Prints and Photographs Division, Library of Congress, 41; Michael Vadon, CC BY-SA 4.0 via Wikimedia Commons, 42

Cherry Lake Press is an imprint of Cherry Lake Publishing Group.

Library of Congress Cataloging-in-Publication Data has been filed and is available at catalog.loc.gov

Printed in the United States of America

CONTENTS

CHAPTER 1

BUILDING A CAMPAIGN TEAM

An election campaign involves a series of political activities. These are meant to **persuade** people to support and vote for a certain candidate. The most well-known campaigns are presidential elections. The media covers them the most. But there are many other political campaigns every year. Members of the House of Representatives are elected every 2 years. Senators serve for 6 years. There are also state, county, and city positions. Most of these elections have some type of campaign.

To help their campaigns run smoothly, candidates create a campaign team. A team for a city-level office may be made up of volunteers. A team for a higher office usually has paid staff members too. Presidential campaigns have

Many people volunteer their time to work on a campaign team leading up to an election.

hundreds of staff members and thousands of volunteers. Everybody works together to try to win the election.

Candidates want to get the best people for their campaign teams. Many staff members are professionals. They have worked on many other campaigns. They may have a lot of experience winning elections.

IN THE OFFICE

Campaign team members do many types of jobs. The leader of the team is the campaign manager. Campaign managers make sure the campaign runs as smoothly as possible. They hire the rest of the staff. They direct the staff's activities each day. They decide how the campaign will spend its money.

Two other staff members help with the campaign **funds**. The finance director is responsible for raising the money for the campaign. They oversee all fundraising events. The campaign treasurer is in charge of the money once it comes in. They record

Campaign managers are in charge of the campaign. They make sure everyone is working to make the campaign successful.

all of the donations. They also keep track of how the money is spent.

The technology manager oversees all technology projects. They handle any computer problems. They create and update the candidate's website. They keep track of all the information used by the campaign.

Many people do a lot of different things at the campaign headquarters. The office manager keeps everything organized. They direct other staff members when necessary. They solve any problems that may arise.

Field directors may hold events in the community to reach voters. They try to spread awareness about their candidate.

IN THE COMMUNITY

Some staff members are more involved in the community. The field director is in charge of contacting voters. They work closely with another staff member, the volunteer coordinator. The volunteer coordinator organizes the volunteers. Volunteers go from house to house to talk with voters. They also call or text voters.

The political director is another member of the staff. They work with certain groups in the community. They help these groups get involved in the campaign. The groups can include seniors, college students, teachers, or **veterans**. They might also include **minority groups**. The political director and the groups figure out ways to reach out to more voters.

Some staff members work in communications. They help spread the campaign's message. They write speeches for the candidate. They also place ads on television, radio, and the internet. Some staff works with social media. They write posts. They keep in touch with voters online.

The head of the communications staff is the communications director. They are sometimes called the press secretary. They are the official spokesperson for the campaign. They set up interviews for the candidate. They answer questions from reporters.

Having an organized schedule is important for a campaign. Schedulers work behind the scenes to get the word out.

The scheduler finds events for the candidate to attend. Then they create a schedule for the candidate. Events can include rallies and fundraisers. They can include visits to towns and colleges. They might include interviews or other television appearances.

As the election gets closer, there is more and more work to do. Some members work all day. Others work all night. They are under a lot of pressure until the election day. But many staff members enjoy the excitement of elections.

FUN FACTS: A STEP AHEAD

Many campaigns have an advance person. The advance person travels to events before the candidate. They set up everything before the candidate arrives. For example, they set up stages for speeches. They get all of the signs in place. They make sure the lighting is good. They will even find just the right people to smile for photos.

CHAPTER 2

CAMPAIGN SIGNS AND SLOGANS

Candidates try different methods to reach voters. These include using campaign signs. A campaign sign is a poster or sign to show support for a candidate.

Candidates also use slogans. A slogan is a phrase that sums up what the candidate stands for. It is usually a short, catchy phrase. It should catch a voter's attention. When used well, signs and slogans can help candidates win more votes.

CAMPAIGN SIGNS

Candidates began using campaign signs in the United States in the 1800s. These early signs were posters. Some included drawings of the candidates. Many of them had a lot of words. Sometimes the text described the candidate. Other times it described important parts of their **platform**.

From school board members to presidents, everyone uses campaign signs when they're running in a public election.

Over time, the technology for printing the signs improved. The signs became more colorful. They included photos of the candidates. Today, many political signs are yard signs. They are printed on plastic. They often have just the candidate's name and the office they are running for on them.

Candidates at every level use campaign signs. They hope the signs will help them win votes. Candidates and their teams place signs along streets and in neighborhoods. The signs remind people of the candidates and their platforms.

Campaign signs are also a way for voters to show support. Voters can display the signs of the candidate

People love to show their support for their preferred candidates on their lawns.

they like best. They place the signs on their lawns and or in their windows.

Signs are especially important for candidates who are not well-known. They place their signs along busy streets. People who drivc past read the signs. They see the candidate's name again and again. They begin to remember it. This is called name recognition. The voters may not know much about the candidate. But they recognize their name on the **ballot**. This can be enough to win the vote.

There are usually many yard signs near polling places. However, there are laws in some states that say how close the signs can be to these locations.

Some of the best signs are the simplest. They show the candidate's name. They might show a photo or a slogan. Voters driving by can read them easily. If there is too much information, people may not pay attention.

SLOGANS

People can find slogans everywhere. Stores, restaurants, and businesses use them. Slogans try to get people to buy certain products. Candidates use slogans in the same way. They try to attract voters.

Some slogans focus on the candidates. They may try to show that the candidate is a regular person. They may point out the candidate's honesty or experience. They may show what the candidate has accomplished. In 1916, President Woodrow Wilson ran for reelection. The United States had not entered World War I (1914–1918) yet. His slogan was "He kept us out of war."

Some slogans express the mood or feelings of the voters. For example, in 1932, many people were

Franklin D. Roosevelt won the 1932 election and continued asking for support for the New Deal programs throughout his presidency.

suffering. They had lost their jobs, homes, and farms. They wanted change and fairness. Franklin D. Roosevelt's slogan was "A New Deal for the American People."

A slogan can also just be a catchy phrase. Dwight Eisenhower's nickname was Ike. In 1952, he ran for president. His slogan was "I like Ike." It was simple and easy to remember. He easily won the election. Four years later, Eisenhower ran and won again. His new slogan was "I still like Ike."

Barack Obama showed that a slogan can be just one word. In 2008, one of his slogans was "Hope." It made people feel that things would get better. An artist created an image of Obama with the slogan underneath it. It became an important symbol in American culture.

Slogans have been placed on many products. These include bumper stickers and T-shirts. Slogans

Obama's single-word slogan was very effective. He won the presidential election in 2008.

can be found on pens and even in fortune cookies. At events, voters often chant the slogan to show support. Some slogans work better than others. They are easier to remember. But the best slogans motivate people to vote.

TRUE STORY: THE BEN GRIFFIN EXPERIMENT

In 2011, a professor named Cindy Kam co-authored a study with Elizabeth Zechmeister. Kam wondered about yard signs. She wanted to find out how much they helped with name recognition. She made up a candidate for a county council election. She gave him the name Ben Griffin. She put up signs for him on a busy street near a school.

A few days later, Kam sent out a **survey** to parents. She asked them which candidate they would vote for. She listed five real candidates, Ben Griffin, and another made-up name. Almost 25 percent of the parents listed Ben Griffin as one of their top choices. The parents had seen Ben's name on the signs. That was enough to win him votes.

CHAPTER 3

CAMPAIGNING WITH TECHNOLOGY

Technology is always changing. As it changes, campaigns change too. Campaigns first used the internet in 1996. This is when the first presidential websites appeared online. The first online donations were made in 1998. Since then, technology continues to affect elections. As technology improves, campaigns can create better strategies.

For example, candidates rely on polls for information. Polls are surveys used to gather voters' opinions. These used to be done by phone. Candidates studied the polls to see how their campaigns were doing. Then they had to figure out what they should change. Today, campaigns use computers to help with this process. They can gather the information more quickly. It is easier to decide what changes to make. This helps candidates get more votes, funds, and support.

Some people feel closer to a candidate when they follow them on social media. This can help the candidate win votes.

Social media has changed elections too. It has become a part of every campaign. Candidates use social media to communicate directly with people. They can create videos to share their own news. They can chat with voters.

FINDING VOTERS

Campaigns use technology to collect a lot of data about voters. This data is information in digital form. This means that it can be stored and used by computers.

The main source of this data is voting records. These tell how people voted in the past. A voting record includes a voter's name and address. It includes which party they belong to. It also lists their birthdate and age.

Most campaigns get data from companies too. The companies gather the data from other sources. Some of the data are just guesses. These may be based on someone's name or where they live. Then the companies sell the data to the campaigns. Campaigns add it to their own data.

Campaigns use the data to figure out strategy. For example, the data can help them understand which issues are most important to voters. The campaign can then **target** certain voters. They can contact the voters who care about those issues. Some voters may not have decided who to support. This can help win their votes. In a close race, these voters could decide who wins the election.

There are many ways to target voters. Campaigns use text messages and phone calls. They use email and social media. Sometimes targeting voters doesn't change the way they vote. But it is another way to collect more data.

People post misinformation on social media to mislead voters. Always check your facts!

PROBLEMS ONLINE

Campaigns are also facing some new challenges because of technology. For example, anyone with an account can post on social media. They can even post false information. This can change people's view of a candidate. The candidate may lose votes because of information that was not true.

During an election, people watch the candidates closely. They pay attention to the things they say and do. They also watch their family members. But now technology allows people to watch candidates even more closely. Most people carry smartphones. Whatever a candidate does or says, someone nearby is likely to record them.

A candidate's actions aren't just reported in the news. Social media shows them on all the different platforms. Videos of the candidates and their families can be played over and over again. Videos are hard to remove once they are on the internet.

Anyone with a smartphone can take pictures or videos and almost immediately post them online. They do this with political candidates.

AI technology allows people to alter images, videos, and audio and make them appear real.

Another problem with social media involves artificial intelligence, or AI. This computer software is designed to work like a human mind. It can spread false information on social media. For example, it can produce fake photos and videos that seem real. Voters may think they are true. AI may cause them to change their votes.

Almost everyone uses social media. People can fact-check what they read about elections.

Technology helps campaigns reach voters. People can share views in many places online. But technology can also be used in harmful ways. The government, online companies, and voters must work hard to make sure elections are protected.

TRUE STORY: TOP SECRET

Campaign teams often have secret projects with code names. During the 2012 election, Barack Obama's campaign created a new way to gather data. Then they used the technology to combine information about voters and volunteers. They called it Project Narwhal. It was named after a whale with one long tusk.

Obama's opponent was Mitt Romney. His campaign began creating a secret program too. They called it the Orca Project. Orcas are killer whales. They attack narwhals. Romney thought his program would be better. But Orca didn't work well on election day.

CHAPTER 4

CAMPAIGN ADS

Election campaigns rely a lot on advertisements, or ads. These messages seek support for a candidate. Through the ads, candidates can reach voters who may not know much about them. They can build name recognition. They can call attention to important issues. They can help raise funds.

There are many types of ads. They may be billboards or other signs. They may be newspaper ads and articles. Brochures, flyers, and letters are ads mailed directly to the voters. Campaigns also run ads on radio, TV, and the internet. The cost of all these advertisements adds up. Altogether, candidates spend billions of dollars on ads.

Rules and laws apply to campaign ads. Some laws are about what the ads include. For example, the name of

A candidate's party is often listed on all official advertising materials. Though it may be in the fine print.

the person or organization who sponsors the ad must be listed. States have other laws too. Candidates should know the rules before they place any ads.

NEGATIVE ADS

Some ads talk about the candidate's good qualities. They may focus on their character or

Some people say they don't respect negative campaigning.

In the 2016 U.S. presidential election, Donald Trump used negative campaigning against Hillary Clinton. He won the election.

accomplishments. The ads try to persuade voters to choose the candidate. But many ads use a different strategy. They try to get voters not to choose the candidate's **opponent**. They do this by telling something unfavorable about the opponent. Some even seem to attack the opponent. These are called negative ads.

Some candidates use more negative ads than positive ones. This is because they work better. Voters remember negative ads more. It is very hard to forget a negative idea. One of the most negative presidential races was in 2012. Almost 70 percent of ads were negative.

Some negative ads make people feel angry. Studies have found that anger motivates voters more than any other feeling. So campaigns create ads that make people angry at the candidate's opponent. They believe more of their supporters will get out and vote.

THE GOOD AND BAD OF SOCIAL MEDIA

The first presidential candidate to use social media ads was Barack Obama in 2008. Since then, social media has changed many things about advertising. Candidates can do more than just place an ad. Now they can connect directly to voters. They can talk about their ideas. They can discuss issues. Or they can just share campaign photos. Social media is cheaper than other forms of advertising. It has become one of the main ways candidates advertise today.

After Obama's successful 2008 social media campaign, other politicians started following suit.

Campaigns use data to find voters and support. They use the data for placing ads on social media too. The ads target certain voters. By using the data, they can show these voters only the ads that matter to them. That way, the ads feature issues the voters care about.

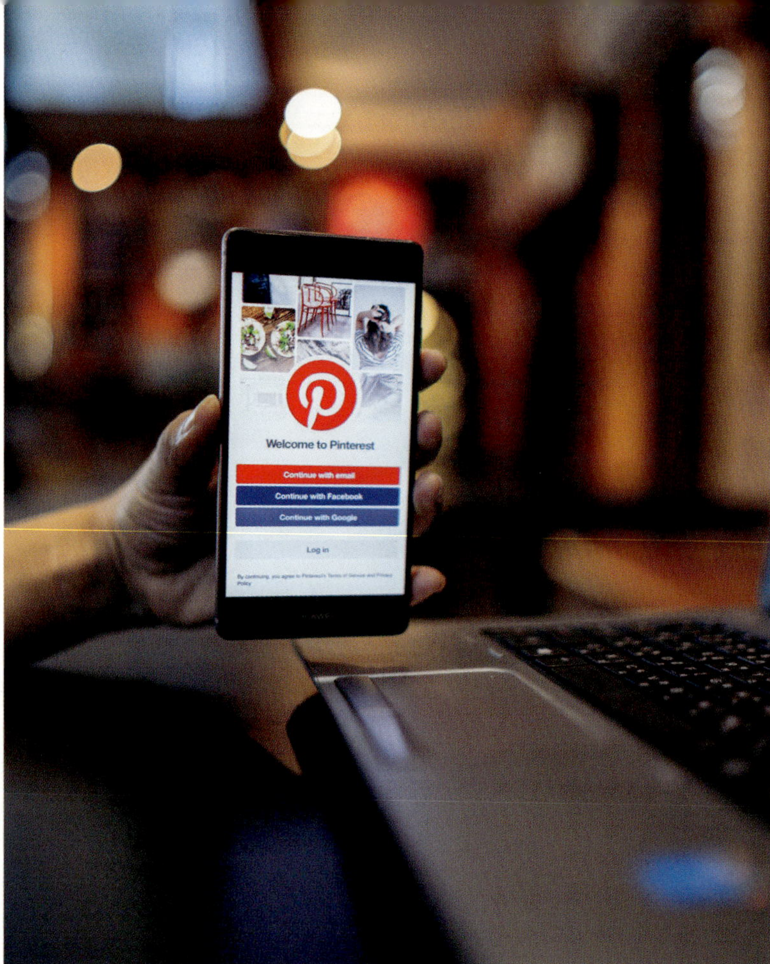

Pinterest is one of the social media platforms that has banned political ads.

But many people don't like targeted campaign ads. They don't think the campaigns should have their personal information. They don't want the campaigns to know about their private lives.

Another problem is that ads on social media aren't always true. Like social media posts, ads can spread a lot of false information. Social media platforms are treated differently than newspapers and TV stations. They don't have to follow the same rules. For this reason, some social media platforms no longer allow political ads.

PERSPECTIVES: STAR POWER

Sometimes celebrities will **endorse** a candidate. They might create posts for social media. They may produce an ad for television or the internet. They tell who they are voting for and why. They hope to affect the way people see certain issues.

But voters don't just follow celebrities, even those they really like. For example, in 2008, TV host Oprah Winfrey endorsed Barack Obama for president. Sixty-nine percent of people polled said that Winfrey's endorsement would not affect their vote. Obama won the election, but Winfrey's endorsement didn't make a difference. Singer Taylor Swift endorsed two candidates for Congress in 2018. But her candidates didn't win. Celebrities who usually focus on issues seem to have more impact.

CHAPTER 5

THE CAMPAIGN TRAIL

Presidential elections always take place in November during an election year. Many candidates announce that they are running about 18 months earlier. This gives them time to try to gain votes. The candidates work with their campaign teams. They come up with a strategy. Part of this strategy is going on a campaign trail.

A campaign trail is the route a candidate takes to talk to people around the country. Candidates travel to different cities and towns. They meet with people face-to-face at the campaign trail stops. They answer people's questions. They explain why they deserve people's votes.

THE TRAIL TO THE TOP

Primary elections begin in January of the election year. The campaign trail then becomes very busy.

The first primary election of the year is always in New Hampshire, after the Iowa caucuses.

Candidates make many stops to try to raise support. They want to get as many votes as they can during the primary elections.

Any location can be a stop. Restaurants and diners are favorite stops for many candidates. The candidates go there to have a meal. Voters come out to meet them.

Many candidates add churches to their list of stops. They may go on Sunday for the church service.

They shake hands with people afterward. Other popular stops include schools and colleges. Candidates talk with the students and teachers. They may visit senior centers. They even meet voters at people's homes.

Other stops include stores and shops. Candidates walk downtown. They meet the voters one-on-one. They have quick chats with people. They sign autographs and pose for selfies.

Some places have become traditional stops. For example, the Red Arrow Diner restaurant chain is a

Presidential candidates usually make a stop at the Red Arrow Diner during New Hampshire's primary.

Donald Trump has signed many "Make America Great Again" hats when he's met with voters.

traditional stop in New Hampshire. Voters can expect candidates to eat and talk with them there. Some places are favorites of just one party. Republicans like to visit Pizza Ranch restaurants in Iowa. Democrats visit Raygun T-shirt shops to meet their Iowa supporters.

The stops are also opportunities for candidates to talk about issues. A candidate might give a short speech in a restaurant or out on the street. They answer questions from voters. The candidates also attend organized events. They participate in rallies and town meetings. Some even visit radio shows to answer questions.

The candidates are not alone on the campaign trail. Members of their campaign team travel with them. At each stop, photographers and reporters are there with cameras. This provides good **publicity** for the candidates.

Candidates and their teams decide how many stops they will make. President Harry S. Truman made a lot of stops to win a second term. In 1948, his

Harry S. Truman's 1948 presidential campaign was successful. He remained president until 1953.

campaign trail included a 31,000-mile (50,000-kilometer) train ride. He gave a total of 352 speeches.

KEY STATES

Each party will have one candidate in the general election. The votes in the primaries decide who the candidates will be. If a candidate wins, their campaign trail will continue. If they lose, the trail will end.

In the United States, each state gets a certain number of votes for president. These are called electoral votes. The number depends on how many people live in the state. When people in a state vote, one candidate wins

In the 2016 presidential election, Hillary Clinton won the popular vote, but Donald Trump won the electoral vote. This meant that Trump won the election.

more votes. That candidate usually gets all of that state's electoral votes. Each state has a set number of electoral votes to be used in the **Electoral College**. The final results of the Electoral College vote help determine the winner of the presidential election.

Some states have more Democrats voting. Some have more Republicans. The candidates know which states they will probably win. But there are some states that could go either way. The race is close in these states. They are called battleground or swing states. These states may change with each election.

Before the general election, the candidates focus on these states. Most of their stops and events take place in these states. If they can win them, it may help them win the election.

SPOTLIGHT ON: THE IOWA STATE FAIR

The Iowa State Fair is held every summer. For many candidates, it is an early stop on the campaign trail. Iowa holds the first presidential primary event in January. It gives voters an idea of who may become the party's candidate.

The fair lasts 11 days. More than 1 million people might attend. Candidates can shake hands with voters. They may give a short speech or an interview. They also take part in traditional fair events. They grill pork chops. They view a life-size cow made of butter. The fair is a good opportunity for candidates to appeal to Iowa voters.

ACTIVITY

CREATE A CATCHY SLOGAN

Choose a friend you think would make a good class president. Now, imagine you are part of their campaign team. It's your job to create their campaign slogan. What would their slogan be?

Before you create a slogan, you'll need some information. Find some supplies for taking notes. Then ask your friend the following questions:

- What is their opinion on serious issues in your school? These might include bullying, peer pressure, or stress.
- What is their opinion on less serious issues in your school? These could include things like being able to eat in class or length of time between classes.
- What other things are important to them?

Write down your friend's answers.

Next, answer the following questions yourself:

- What are your friend's positive characteristics? Are they honest? Caring? Kind? Strong? Brave? Determined?
- What makes your friend unique?
- What skills or talents does your friend have?
- What makes them a great friend?

Review famous campaign slogans to give you inspiration. For example:

A Square Deal for All – *Taft Campaign 1908*
Build Back Better – *Biden Campaign 2020*
I Like Ike – *Eisenhower Campaign 1952*
It's Morning Again in America – *Reagan Campaign 1984*
Make America Great Again – *Trump Campaign 2016*
Yes We Can – *Obama Campaign 2008*

Next, use this information to write down some slogan ideas. Slogans are usually short, so each one will probably focus on just one thing from your list. For example, you could write a slogan that focuses on a certain issue. You could write one that focuses on a characteristic. Or you could write one that is just fun to say. Write down as many slogan ideas as you can think of.

Show the slogans to your friend. Together, choose your favorite slogan.

Rewrite the slogan as you might see it on a poster or bumper sticker. Be sure to include your friend's name. You can also add drawings or graphics to make it stand out.

GLOSSARY

Electoral College (ih-LEK-tuh-ruhl KAA-lij) part of the U.S. presidential elections; process in which electors from each state vote for president and vice president

endorse (in-DORS) to support or approve something

funds (FUHNDZ) money set aside for a certain purpose

minority groups (MUH-nohr-uh-tee GROOPS) smaller groups in a population, often based on characteristics such as race or religion

opponent (uh-POH-nuhnt) a person who is competing against another person

persuade (per-SWAYD) to influence someone's beliefs or actions through communication and reasoning

platform (PLAT-form) a set of ideas and views on important issues promoted by a political party or candidate

primary elections (PRIE-mehr-ee uh-LEK-shuhnz) elections within a political party where members choose their candidate for the general election

publicity (puh-BLIH-suh-tee) information intended to attract public interest

survey (SER-vay) a collection of information on a particular subject from a certain group of people

target (TAHR-guht) to direct efforts toward specific groups to better connect with their interests

veterans (VEH-tuh-ruhnz) people who have served in the military

TO LEARN MORE

BOOKS

Berne, Emma Carlson. *Election Campaigns: A Kid's Guide.* North Mankato, MN: Capstone, 2020.

Kogler, Peter. *Political Campaigns*. New York: Cavendish Square Publishing, 2021.

Thorpe, Judy. *What Are Political Campaigns?* New York: Kidhaven Press, 2022.

WEBSITES

Search these online sources with an adult:

"America 101: Why Do Candidates Use Campaign Slogans?" History.com.

"Hit the Campaign Trail." Louisiana's Old State Capitol Museum of Political History.

"Win the White House." ICivics.org.

INDEX

ABOUT THE AUTHOR

Samantha Bell was born and raised near Orlando, Florida. She grew up in a family of eight kids and all kinds of pets, including goats, chickens, cats, dogs, rabbits, horses, parakeets, hamsters, guinea pigs, a monkey, a raccoon, and a coatimundi. She now lives with her family in the foothills of the Blue Ridge Mountains, where she enjoys hiking, painting, and snuggling with their cats, Pocket, Pebble, and Mr. Tree-Tree Triggers.